RAILWAYS

of the

PEAK DISTRICT

Compiled by
MICHAEL BLAKEMORE
and
DAVID MOSLEY

In the same series:
RAILWAYS OF THE YORKSHIRE DALES
RAILWAYS OF THE NORTH YORK MOORS

Atlantic Publishers
Trevithick House, West End, Penryn, Cornwall TR10 8HE

ISBN; 1 902827 09 0

© ATLANTIC PUBLISHERS 2003

Printed by THE AMADEUS PRESS LTD., BRADFORD

British Cataloguing in Publication Data
A catalogue for this book is available from the British Library

CONTENTS

An atmospheric moment in time captured at Hope station in April 1965 as the guard of the 17.30 from Sheffield to Manchester Central shows a green flag to the driver of LMS Class 5 No.44888. A clear starting signal beckons the train on to run round the flank of Lose Hill. (Dr. L.A. Nixon)

INTRODUCTION

The Peak District — a misnomer if ever there was one as the area boasts few pointed hills and, rising to 2,088ft at its highest point on Kinder Scout, cannot really be considered to be mountainous. Forming the southern extremity of the Pennine Chain, the Peak District is rather a high, breezy, limestone plateau, country "hollow like a drum" according to Conan Doyle, riven by caverns and quarries and cut by secretive valleys through which flow clear rivers with gentle names like Lathkill, Wye and Dove. To the west, north and east of the limestone plateau is a forbidding horseshoe of gritstone edges and moorlands with Derbyshire's major river, the Derwent, cutting a path between White and Dark Peaks down the eastern side.

The Peak has been long settled by man; prehistoric monuments at Arbor Low and on Stanton Moor are evidence of this. The Romans prized the area for its lead and in the Dark Ages Bakewell was an important northern outpost of Mercia. The Normans used the area as a hunting preserve — the Peak Forest with its Chapel-en-le-Frith and the whole guarded by Peveril Castle at Castleton. As the Middle Ages waned, so the great houses at Hardwick, Haddon and Chatsworth established themselves although the old fears returned with an outbreak of the Plague at Eyam in 1666. Even before this inquisitive visitors had begun to penetrate the Peak; in 1653 Isaak Walton in *The Compleat Angler* wrote in praise of Dovedale but in 1725 Daniel Defoe called the limestone uplands "a howling wilderness".

In 1771, at Cromford, Richard Arkwright brought the Industrial Revolution to the Peak District. The Peak had always had industry; lead mining, with its arcane traditions, had flourished from Roman times and the work of 't'owd man' is inscribed all over the face of the land. From the quarries came the millstones to grind flour – so much so that the very rock is named 'millstone grit' – but Arkwright brought the factory system and took advantage of the Peak District's abundant waterpower to produce cotton cloth. Cromford became one of the first industrial villages and the gaunt mills soon spread through the Derbyshire valleys.

Now transport was found wanting; pack horses were not suited to factory production volumes and the canals, Cromford in the south east and Peak Forest to the north west, could only touch the hilly fringes. It would be up to the developing railways

to carry goods to and through the Peak District to ensure that industry prospered. In this book we briefly survey how railways were built into, through, over and under the Peak District not only to open up its industrial prospects to the outside world but also to provide vital links between the northern towns of Lancashire and Yorkshire, the East Midlands and ultimately London. And what a fascinating network was eventually created — ranging from the horse-worked Peak Forest Tramway to the Midland Railway's important Derby to Manchester main line, from the eccentric Cromford & High Peak line which clambered up, down and around the landscape to avoid massive civil engineering to the Hope Valley route which boasted Britain's second longest tunnel, from two competing routes to serve the prospering spa town of Buxton to a couple of narrow gauge curiosities built to tap the industries of fringe valleys.

The opening up of the Peak District to railway communication also brought another form of traffic which was to be of increasing importance — the pleasure traveller. In the latter part of the nineteenth century people in towns and cities began turning to the countryside for fresh air and healthy exercise. There was a particularly strong movement in northern industrial areas to form rambling clubs, such as the Manchester YMCA Rambling Club in 1880 and the Midland Institute of Ramblers in 1894. These in turn led to larger federations — the Manchester Ramblers Council was set up in 1919, the Liverpool & District Federation in 1922 and the Sheffield & District Federation in 1926. By the 1930s there was a need for a national body to represent rambling interests and a meeting in the already popular Peak District at Longshaw in 1931 laid the foundations for the National Council of Ramblers Federations.

However, not everyone welcomed ramblers and the landowners were often hostile to the idea of allowing access to farmland and grouse moors. This came to a head with a mass trespass on Kinder Scout in 1932, resulting in a number of arrests and prison sentences. Nevertheless the creation of the Ramblers Association in 1935 saw it become a major campaigner for the establishment of national parks of which the Peak National Park was the first, in 1951.

For many years railways were instrumental in bringing visitors into the Peak District to enjoy its beauty but in more recent times the volume of car ownership has generated growing problems of overcrowded roads, parking and environmental intrusion. Today there is widespread awareness of the role public transport can play in reducing car usage, so helping to safeguard this priceless natural asset.

So what railway legacy has been left to the Peak District? Inevitably, the decline of the rural branch line has affected the area, with the Ashbourne and Wirksworth routes (along with the two narrow gauge curios) closing long before Dr. Beeching came on the scene. The Doctor's fortunes were mixed and produced some surprising results — the Stockport to Buxton line was fought for and saved but, extraordinarily, the mighty Midland's main line was axed between Matlock and Chinley. The loss of a direct route between Manchester and the East Midlands still seems inexplicable, especially given that part of it remains used by limestone traffic — but there has been talk of reviving it. In the meantime what was once part of an important main line now languishes only as a single track byway between Ambergate and its terminus at Matlock. The Hope Valley line is another survivor and, perhaps against the odds, became the only link between Manchester and Sheffield when the electrified Woodhead route was abandoned in 1981.

Some of the lost routes — the Ashbourne branch, the Cromford & High Peak and the Leek & Manifold — can still be enjoyed by walkers and those who trespassed on Kinder or who formed the thriving Ramblers Association would have been pleased at the access they now offer. The Peak District remains an area of industrial, railway and scenic delight which should certainly be visited.

The authors would like to acknowledge the help of those who have generously provided photographs for this book, in particular John Edgington, Gavin Morrison, Michael Mensing, Les Nixon, John Morten and Bob Essery.

Michael Blakemore
David Mosley
November 2002

THE MIDLAND MAIN LINE

The Midland Railway main line through the Peak District was never intended as a railway by-way; indeed it was always one of the company's principal main lines linking the East Midlands with the industrial North West and St. Pancras with Manchester Central. But the railway events of the 1960s conspired against the line and it was severed by the 'Beeching Axe' in 1968.

All that remains today is, from the south, a short passenger branch of the national network linking Ambergate and Matlock. This is continued up the Derwent valley as far as Rowsley by the preservationists of Peak Rail. In the north a freight-only line comes from Chinley and through the Dove Holes Tunnel to link the limestone quarries above Buxton with the chemical industries of the Cheshire Plain. This line still uses Dove Holes Tunnel, the allegedly unsafe condition of which was one of the most pressing reasons for the line's closure as a through route in the 1960s.

What became the Midland main line through the Peak began life as a small railway with an expansive title and powerful friends in high places. Supported by George Stephenson, now — in his later years — living at nearby Chesterfield, the 'Railway King' himself George Hudson and George Henry Cavendish MP of Chatsworth, the Manchester, Buxton, Matlock & Midlands Junction Railway opened from Ambergate — on the North Midland line — as far as Rowsley, eleven miles up the Derwent valley through the Matlocks, on 4th June 1849.

And there it rested, a victim of aristocratic debate and railway politicking. Should the line go on towards Manchester up the Derwent valley and through His Grace the Duke of Devonshire's estate at Chatsworth or up the Wye valley and through the Rutland estate at Haddon? Or should it go towards Manchester at all? Not if the London & North Western had its way — the 'Premier Line' wished to keep as much of the Manchester traffic for itself as possible and it used its large shareholding in the MBM&MJR to check Midland ambitions, this in spite of the Midland having worked the MBM&MJR since its opening!

After the usual round of posturing, proposal and counter-proposal, in 1860 the Midland was authorized to extend the line

from Rowsley north westwards to Buxton. The line traversed the Duke of Rutland's estate at Haddon where a cut and cover tunnel screened the steam and smoke from the Duke's view. Five men were killed in this folly and the Midland was forced to provide £100 in compensation to the relatives of the dead men. At Bakewell a suitably aristocratic station met the Duke's needs and served the townspeople while the next station, Hassop, allowed passengers for Chatsworth to alight in appropriate style. The line continued on a gradient of about 1 in 100 under Monsal Head, leapt across the Wye on the Monsal Head Viaduct and followed the side of the gorge as far as Miller's Dale. Here the Buxton line made its way up Ashwood Dale to reach the breezy spa town. The line opened on 1st June 1863 but not everyone was as pleased as the Midland's directors. John Ruskin, the artist and writer, saw pre-Midland Monsal Dale as an abode of the gods and regarded the coming of the railway as vandalism of the very worst sort: "You enterprised a Railroad through the valley, you blasted its rocks away, heaped thousands of tons of shale into its lovely stream. The valley is gone, and the Gods with it: and now, every fool in Buxton can be at Bakewell in half an hour, and every fool in Bakewell at Buxton — you Fools everywhere".

From Miller's Dale Junction the Manchester line climbed away up Great Rocks Dale on a gradient of 1 in 90 for three miles. Just over the summit, 985 feet above sea level, it entered the great tunnel at Dove Holes. At 2,984 yards long, Dove Holes Tunnel provided a test of civil engineers and footplatemen alike. During construction an underground river was twice encountered but despite this, work was completed in three years and freight traffic began to pass through the tunnel in the autumn of 1866. The tunnel gained a reputation for mishap. A landslip in 1872 forced a month's closure and three month's traffic was forfeited in 1904 by a rockfall at the Manchester end of the tunnel. There was a further collapse in 1940 and in severe winters icicles formed an additional hazard, hanging down from the tunnel's roof and portals. It was not unknown for a light engine to be dispatched as an icebreaker — and despite all, the tunnel remains open, passing the heaviest trains in its history!

From Dove Holes Tunnel the line descends at 1 in 90 for about five miles to Chinley. In due time a junction was formed here with the Hope Valley line and the station became a focal point for Midland connections to Liverpool and north east Lancashire. The Midland was at first reliant on other companies for access into Manchester but in July 1880 the Cheshire Lines Committee, of which the MR was part-owner, opened its new terminus at Manchester Central.

A service to London which had taken five hours in 1868 was, by the outbreak of World War I, reduced to 3 hours 35 minutes, causing the London & North Western and the Great Central Railways to look to their laurels. Hauled by a developing succession of 2-4-0s, 4-4-0s and eventually the elegant 4-4-0 Compounds, Midland expresses modestly offered 'The Best Way' from Manchester to the capital. The Midland was, of course, the pioneer of improvements in third class travel — decent carriages for all!

The Peak line also proved to be a principal freight artery. Midland 0-6-0s slogged over the gable at Dove Holes whilst marshalling yards at Rowsley and Gowhole, just on the Manchester side of Chinley, shuffled and dealt out again the various traffics of the East Midlands and the North West. In London, Midland & Scottish days the Stanier 8F 2-8-0s took an increasing part in freight haulage over the Peak and in British Railways days the splendid 9F 2-10-0s were a common sight.

By LMS days express passenger trains had graduated to 4-6-0 haulage, 'Jubilees' and 'Black 5s' to the fore. 1938 saw the line boast two named trains, the 10.00am Manchester Central—St. Pancras becoming 'The Palatine' and the up 4.25pm 'The Peak Express'. Towards the end of steam larger locomotives, 'Royal Scot' 4-6-0s and 'Britannia' Pacifics, appeared on the best trains and, appropriately enough, it was left to the 'Peak' class diesel-electrics (Classes 45 and 46) to play out the final chapter.

Ironically the line was as busy in its last decade as at any time in its history. The electrification of the former LNWR route from London to Manchester brought extra traffic by way of diverted trains. Between 1960 and 1966 the vivid blue, all first class, six-car, diesel 'Midland Pullman' brought a flash of light to the twilight days — and a London to Manchester travelling time of 3 hours 10 minutes.

But the end was in sight. Rowsley sidings closed in 1964 when freight traffic was diverted away from the line. Local services between Matlock and Chinley ceased in March 1967 and 'express' services finished on 1st July 1968.

North of Rowsley and south of Great Rocks Dale the line now slumbers as a cycle or walkway — awaiting a revival as a preserved line or as once again an integral part of the national railway network?

Matlock Bath station photographed in July 1889. Still a popular resort for trippers, Matlock Bath was referred to as 'the Switzerland of England' – hence the chalet style for the station. The entrance to High Tor No.1 Tunnel can be seen in the background and much of the next mile and a half to Matlock is travelled in four tunnels. (NRM/DY 3135)

At Ambergate the main line over the Peak left the former North Midland route. A remarkable triangular station developed with the up Peak line using Platform 2 and the original down Derby to Chesterfield route taking Platform 3. At 3 o'clock in the Edwardian era the station staff are out in force and the railway cottages to the right of the picture could have been rented from the Midland Railway for 4s (20p) a week. (Pendragon collection)

Cromford station in 1911 and Midland Compound No.1021 roars through with a Derby-bound express. This rather grand small station reflected Cromford's links with the industrial Arkwrights and in the 1870s the booking office sold an average of 70 tickets a day. That an elegant Midland express was a 1911 commonplace is evidenced by the man on the right who is engrossed in his newspaper! (NRM/DY 9561)

Railway byway or main line in waiting? At present Peak Rail is a pleasant preserved railway using the trackbed of the former Midland main line and linking the outskirts of Matlock with the south end of what were the marshalling yards at Rowsley. Peak Rail describes itself as ' The Matlock and Buxton Railway Project' and long-term ambitions involve reuniting the Peak District towns by rail. In the Peak Rail present, these pictures show a train leaving the Rowsley end of the line; the thick stand of trees behind the train marks the site of the former Rowsley loco depot. The two 0-6-0ST locomotives masquerading as Class J94 are appropriate. Nos.68006 and 68012 were Rowsley engines at the end of steam days and spent their service either in the marshalling yard or on the Cromford & High Peak line. (Peak Rail)

Although the author was trainspotting at York on 11th April 1964, when this photograph was taken it was business as usual at Matlock as LMS 8F 2-8-0 No.48673 approached the station with a rake of mineral wagons returning to the East Midlands coalfield. At present this location is the ' no-man's-land' between the national network and Peak Rail but the preserved railway has high hopes of a return to Matlock station within the next couple of years. (Alan Tyson collection)

A tranquil view of Rowsley station at the turn of the last century. The line to Manchester is climbing towards the camera on a gradient of 1 in 102. Just visible behind the station nameboard, which is favoured with a full-stop, can be seen the roof of the original engine shed at the terminus of the Manchester, Buxton, Matlock & Midlands Junction Railway. (NRM/DY 2452)

BR 'Peak' (later Class 46) 1Co-Co1 No.D157 heads south of Matlock with a Manchester Central to London St. Pancras express on 16th June 1962. At the start of the 1960s these powerful diesel-electrics began to displace the 'Jubilees', 'Royal Scots' and 'Britannias' on Midland main line expresses. (Cliff Woodhead)

Midland main line or Matlock branch? In January 1986 the train to Derby, formed by one of the then prototype Metropolitan-Cammell 'Sprinter'-type units, stands at the truncated remains of Matlock station. These units, designated Class 151, were, as the author recalls, comfortable and stylish and so were almost inevitably destined for a short life! (Author's collection)

From Rowsley banking assistance was provided for freight trains on the sixteen-mile climb to Peak Forest. Here 8F 2-8-0 No.48327 pounds upgrade through Chee Dale...

...aided and abetted in the rear by 2-6-4T No.42053, whose crew and the guard in the van in front of the locomotive must have been relieved to have emerged from atmosphere in the tunnel behind them!
(Alan Tyson collection)

'The Palatine', the 2.25pm from Manchester Central to St. Pancras, coasts down past Tunstead Quarry Sidings towards its stop at Millers Dale in July 1960. The locomotive is 'Royal Scot' class 4-6-0 No.46162 Queen's Westminster Rifleman. 'Scots' and 'Britannias' were 'big power' for the Peak line and only really began to appear alongside the more familiar 'Jubilees' and 'Black 5s' as the new diesels took over more of their duties on the West Coast Main Line. (Alan Tyson collection)

Short and steep! – about five miles at 1 in 90 from Chinley up to Dove Holes on the southbound climb. 8F 2-8-0 No. 48605 struggles under the embankment carrying the LNWR Buxton line over the Midland as it brings empty hoppers from the chemicals industry of Cheshire back for their refill of best Derbyshire limestone. (Alan Tyson collection)

And now the Gods have gone — to be replaced by an 'Austin 7'. A Fowler 7F 0-8-0 wanders through the delights of Monsal Dale in the high summer of 1956. Even a remote a spot as this merited goods sidings, crossovers and a signal box. (D.A. Kelson/Colour Rail BRM1716)

Peak Forest in 1954. 4F 0-6-0 No.44566 runs down from the summit and through Peak Forest station with a train of empty wagons. (Colour Rail)

Standard portraits – 1. 9F 2-10-0 No.92056 reflects on its progress over Monsal Head Viaduct in June 1961. (Colour Rail)

Standard portraits – 2. 'Britannia' Pacific No.70013 Oliver Cromwell *matches the glorious greens of Cressbrook Dale as it emerges from Litton Tunnel with an end of steam special from St. Pancras on 9th June 1968 which it worked from Derby to Manchester Victoria and back via the Hope Valley to Nottingham.* (P.J. Fitton/Colour Rail)

Peak Forest in April 1989. Two Class 37 locomotives bring a train of roadstone on to what was the Midland main line towards the site of the old Peak Forest station on 7th April 1989. Semaphore signals and a Midland signal box still control operations! (Dr. L.A. Nixon)

Buxton, a spa town with associations going back to Roman times and by the mid-nineteenth century enjoying something of a fashionable revival under the patronage of the Duke of Devonshire, was just the place, reasoned the directors of the Midland Railway, to be on their direct route over the Peak to Manchester. The London & North Western thought differently and it blocked the Midland with a line up to Buxton from Stockport and Whaley Bridge. Both companies opened lines into Buxton on 30th May 1863 but the Midland had to be content with access over a four mile long branch from Millers Dale on its developing Manchester route via Peak Forest. It was perhaps ironic that the rival companies should use adjacent identical twin stations in Buxton. These were designed by Sir Joseph Paxton of Crystal Palace fame and the LNWR half of the station remains in use to this day. The railways stimulated the growth of Buxton; a population of 1,800 in 1861 had risen to over 6,000 by 1881.

Millers Dale station was the key to the Midland services to Buxton. The station served local towns and villages such as Tideswell and Taddington but much of its activity was concerned with the connecting services to and from Buxton. That these might not have been all that passengers had hoped for was exemplified by the *High Peak News* which in November 1900 referred to Millers Dale as 'Patience Junction'. In 1879, however, 'Strephon' — Edward Bradbury, clerk and unofficial publicist for the Midland Railway — caught a much more positive atmosphere in changing at Millers Dale.

"Here Mr. Salford, from Manchester, who has left his rheumatism and crutches behind at Buxton gets nimbly in the express along with Mrs. Salford, and the two Miss Salfords, one a charming symphony in silk, the other a dainty vignette in velvet. Mr. Saltley, of Birmingham, very gouty and bound for Buxton, gets out, and there is an interchange of several other passengers. A stout gentleman, who carries a red nose and a fishing rod, pants pathetically up the platform...he is just one puff too late, and in waiting for the next train he will have time to moralize on the evils of punctuality."

From Millers Dale a Buxton train followed the main line for nearly two miles to Millers Dale Junction. The Buxton line then diverged, passing Blackwell Mill Halt which served the railway cottages contained within the triangle of lines and was a credible contender for the 'smallest station in the world' title. From Buxton Junction the line climbed Ashwood Dale on a gradient of 1 in 100, served a number of quarries and within four miles entered Buxton itself.

Three distinct forms of passenger train could be seen on the line. In both Midland and LMS days a through carriage service was offered from Buxton to London or vice versa. This saved the traveller from having to change trains — the carriage itself being shunted as necessary — and in 1903 a first class return from St. Pancras to Buxton cost £2 3s 4d (£2.17). Local services linked Buxton with Manchester, Chinley, Matlock and Derby but the most frequent trains on the line was the 'shuttle' service to Millers Dale. In Midland days this was typically thirteen trains each way daily, by the LMS period seventeen trains and by the 1960s, immediately before the closure of the line, nineteen trains in both directions each day. From 1956 the Millers Dale services were worked by diesel multiple units, but from 1934 the steam service had been operated in push-pull mode using a fascinating variety of locomotives including Midland 0-4-4Ts and Webb 2-4-2Ts.

Buxton proved a popular destination for excursion traffic, both day trips and evening outings, and the railways proved invaluable communication links when the snow fell. All passenger services ceased on the Midland line on 6th March 1967.

Freight traffic, in the form of limestone trains from the quarries to the south of Buxton, continues to flow over the Midland line. In the 1930s this route carried heavy coal traffic from Sheffield and Rowsley to Buxton — an unlikely location for the coal wagons to be sorted and forwarded into Lancashire, Cheshire and Staffordshire, but a traffic flow which reinforces the all-pervasive nature of the railways.

Steam endured almost to the end in the Peak District and in seasonable February weather in 1968 8F 2-8-0 No.48327 heads for Chinley and then onward to Buxton with empty limestone hoppers.
(Derek Huntriss/Colour Rail BRM1296)

Dappled sunlight adorns Rowsley's 4F o-6-o No.44080 as it waits in Buxton station with a single coach for Millers Dale. The station clock and roofboard indicate that this coach will be attached to the 8.55am (Saturdays excepted) Manchester Central to London St. Pancras at Millers Dale, giving passengers from Buxton an uninterrupted arrival in the capital at 1.07pm (Colour Rail)

Although Millers Dale served the surrounding settlements such as Tideswell, Taddington and Wormhill (the birthplace of James Brindley, the great canal engineer), its principal function was as the junction for Buxton. On a wet day in the early 1930s the scene is pure Midland with Compound 4-4-0 No.1020 on a down stopper and the Buxton branch train headed by No.1366, a Johnson 0-4-4T built in 1892.
(Pendragon collection)

On Easter Monday 1956 the 4.58pm Millers Dale to Buxton service approaches Chee Tor No.1 Tunnel propelled by Stanier 0-4-4T No.41905. Push-pull working was introduced on the branch in the mid-1930s.
(Michael Mensing)

Buxton was served by a number of 'intermediate' distance trains from places such as Chinley, Derby and Matlock. Here a stopper from Derby passes the splitting distants at Millers Dale Junction heading for Buxton on Easter Monday 1956. The locomotive is Ivatt Class 2 2-6-0 No.46440.
(Michael Mensing)

*Ashwood Dale in June 1913 and a Midland
Class 1 2-4-0 heads for Buxton. The road in the
dale is now the A6 – and hardly as quiet!*
(NRM/DY 9786)

Buxton station – Midland side – and in the mid-1950s Johnson 0-4-4T No.58083 (built in 1895) prepares to leave for Millers Dale with a through coach to be attached to the St. Pancras express. (T.J. Edgington collection)

By 1961 the Millers Dale 'shuttles' were diesel multiple units. Here, on 23rd September of that year, a two-car Gloucester Railway Carriage & Wagon Company set forming the 12.05pm from the junction has arrived at Buxton. (Michael Mensing)

Towards the end of the steam era the 5.22pm express from Manchester Central to Buxton achieved something of a reputation as a prestige train. On 22nd May 1951 'Jubilee' class 4-6-0 No.45657 Tyrwhitt *is seen at Topley Pike on the last leg of the journey.* (E.R.Morten)

Midland Compound 4-4-0 No.41103 climbs from Buxton Junction towards Peak Forest Junction with a train for Chinley in October 1957. The train is just about to pass the intriguingly named Cherbourg quarry, opened by the Midland in 1878 to supply its own ballast needs. (E.R. Morten)

Buxton Junction in October 1955 and Fowler 2-6-4T No.42367 runs down to join the line from Millers Dale. The train is giving a pretty good representation of the early British Railways corporate style but the signals protecting the junction remain resolutely Midland. (E.R. Morten)

The station screen on the Midland side at Buxton. Today this area is a road 'improvement', leaving the 'Premier Line' with the last laugh (see page 57). (T.J. Edgington)

THE WIRKSWORTH BRANCH

From October 1867 until its final closure in the late 1980s the Wirksworth branch served its public and its successive owners, the Midland Railway, the London, Midland & Scottish and British Railways in unobtrusive fashion. Limestone from the quarries around Wirksworth and milk from the farms of the Ecclesbourne Valley provided the main outgoing traffic whilst inward came coal, agricultural equipment and supplies and general goods. Four or so passenger trains a day generally catered for the numbers of people travelling, although extra capacity was provided at the time of the Wirksworth well-dressings. Leaving the Midland main line at Duffield trains called at Hazlewood, Shottle and Idridgehay in the course of their rural journey of just over eight miles to Wirksworth.

But it could all have been so different. At its opening the Wirksworth line was seen as a part of a possible Midland main line to Manchester and as such its structures were built with double track in mind. In the early 1860s the Midland Railway was pressing ahead with its line from Rowsley towards Buxton and Manchester. The link from Rowsley to the main Midland system at Ambergate was provided by the Manchester, Buxton, Matlock & Midlands Junction Railway — which the Midland operated but in which its arch-rival, the London & North Western, had a significant interest. It was unthinkable that the Midland line over the Peak would be completed just in time for the rug to be pulled out from underneath as the North Western acquired the MBM&MJR when the lease came up for renewal in 1871!

So the Midland plotted an independent line, up from Duffield to Wirksworth and then, if necessary, on through the amphitheatre of hills overlooking the town, on through the great whale-back of Masson Hill and down to Rowsley, well out of the way of the North Western. Massive tunnelling would have been involved but it was all unnecessary as in due course the line from Ambergate came into the Midland fold.

The Wirksworth line opened with little ceremony in October 1867, the original timetable showing three passenger trains, two 'parliamentaries' and one first and second class, either way each day. By the turn of the century this had increased to four plus two round trips by steam railmotor. The adverse gradients of the branch soon defeated these flimsy machines and an exotic train comprising a Midland & Great Northern Joint Railway tank engine hauling an original 1874 Pullman car replaced them.

A fatal accident marred the branch's tranquil existence. In February 1935 the 8.40pm passenger train from Wirksworth to Derby was derailed near Hazlewood. The driver was killed and the fireman badly scalded. Colonel Trench, investigating, placed the blame firmly on the outdated permanent way. This, consisting of rails of 21ft length, had been laid in 1885 and was not up to the weight of a Derby 'Big Goods' engine at speed.

Services were reduced with the outbreak of the Second World War but it was the coal shortage after the war which put paid to passenger traffic. The last service train ran on 16th June 1947; general goods services survived to feel Dr. Beeching's axe in April 1968 and stone traffic from the quarries ended some fifteen years ago.

The 1950s saw the branch used to commission the whole of Derby Works' output of diesel multiple units, while a splash of colour returned to Wirksworth station on 7th September 1961 in the form of four preserved steam locomotives. The Midland Compound No.1000 towed 'Spinner' 4-2-2 No.118, Kirtley 2-4-0 No.158A and the LTSR 4-4-2T *Thundersley* from Derby to be filmed from the TV series *Railway Roundabout*.

The future seems bright, too. In 2002 WyvernRail launched a share issue aimed at breathing life back into the Wirksworth branch — for commuters and visitors to the Peak and perhaps even freight in the fullness of time. A railway byway revived?

Shottle station looking south. The overbridge bears testament to the Midland Railway's unfulfilled ambition for the Wirksworth branch. In this photograph the station staff confidently outnumber the passenger and the milk churns on the platform might just have come from the author's Uncle Wilf's farm — just over the bridge and turn left.
(R.J. Essery collection)

There's a lot more milk for collection at Idridgehay and no expense has been spared on station buildings, station master's house or signal box. A view looking towards Wirksworth in Midland Railway days.
(R.J. Essery collection)

A view in Midland Railway days of Wirksworth station looking towards the sidings which served the quarries to the north of the town. The location is now that of WyvernRail which is working to reactivate the branch.
(T.J. Edgington collection)

In the immediate post-Second World War years Ivatt Class 2 2-6-2T No.1206 stands at Wirksworth with the 6.07pm service to Derby. The hills in the background represent the first part of the barrier the Midland Railway would have faced in driving a line forward from Wirksworth and on to Rowsley. The price of independence from the LNWR would have been some mighty tunnelling!
(R.J. Essery collection)

THE HOPE VALLEY LINE

Lancashire and Yorkshire — two counties locked in rivalry and between them the great Pennine hills stand as a sort of natural barrier to keep them apart. The Industrial Revolution increased the necessity of improving transport between the great commercial centres developing on either side of the Pennines but the barrier was a difficult one to cross. The Rochdale Canal was completed in 1804, the Huddersfield Canal was fully opened in 1811 with the completion of the Standedge Tunnel, while the Leeds & Liverpool Canal, opened in 1816, took a roundabout route and entered the West Riding through the Aire Gap. However, within a few decades the railways were taking up the challenge of creating direct links between Manchester and places such as Leeds, Bradford, Huddersfield and Sheffield.

The first three great trans-Pennine routes do not feature in the Peak District story but they are not without relevance. The Manchester & Leeds Railway, engineered by George Stephenson, passed through the Summit Tunnel on the Calder Valley route, completed in 1841, followed five years later by the epic Woodhead Tunnel route of the Sheffield, Ashton-under Lyne & Manchester Railway, while the Colne and Tame Valleys were taken by the Huddersfield & Manchester Railway (later LNWR) in 1849, passing under the Pennines at Standedge. Interestingly, the later the railway the longer the tunnel!

The SAMR (later Great Central) might not have been the first route between Sheffield and Manchester. In 1830 a Sheffield & Manchester Railway, with George and Robert Stephenson as engineers, was proposed to connect with the pioneering Liverpool & Manchester Railway. An Act of Parliament was obtained in 1831 but the route sanctioned was a fearsome one involving inclined planes and over six miles of tunnels. At such an early date the engineering enormity of the project was too great and its costs too high and uncertain with the result that it was abandoned before it was begun.

For some 50 years the Woodhead railway route was the only one between Manchester and Sheffield but the powerful Midland Railway, which ran to both cities from the south over two of its most important main lines, was not getting any of the traffic. In 1872 it proposed a route from Dore, south of Sheffield on the main line to Derby, to Hassop, north of Bakewell. Nothing came of this and it was left to the Dore & Chinley Railway to obtain powers in 1884 for what became the Hope Valley route. Again, it was a huge engineering undertaking but in 1888 the MR took it over; the building in the previous decade of the Settle—Carlisle line had left it undaunted!

Construction of the 21-mile Dore & Chinley Line (to give its official name) began in 1888 and such was the mountainous terrain through which it was to be directed that over a quarter of its length was in tunnels. From the junction at Dore the line entered Totley Tunnel, at 3 miles 950 yards the second longest in Britain. This brought the railway into the Hope Valley and the Vale of Edale before it disappeared into Cowburn Tunnel whose 2 miles 182 yards earned it ninth place in the list of longest tunnels. The line opened to goods on 6th November 1893 and to passengers on 1st June 1894.

The Midland now had its own trans-Pennine line which, despite its tunnels, was less formidable in operating terms than the Woodhead route. The Hope Valley line, though, was never as pre-eminent in attracting Manchester—Sheffield passenger traffic as was the Woodhead route, particularly after the latter's electrification in 1954. It did, however, play a very important role in freight haulage, especially of the limestone quarried in the Peak District and of the cement manufactured at Hope.

It has been the unfolding of history over the four three decades which has elevated the Hope Valley's status, beginning in 1968 when the Peak Forest main line between Chinley and Matlock was surprisingly closed to passengers. Next in 1970 the Woodhead route passenger service was withdrawn and Manchester—Sheffield trains were concentrated on the Hope Valley, then the controversial complete closure of the Woodhead route in 1981 brought it more freight traffic. Today the Hope Valley is a busy main line and has become a valuable component of a number of new cross-country itineraries linking Liverpool, Lancashire, the East Midlands, Lincolnshire and East Anglia.

Horsehill Tor soars above the eastern end of Cowburn Tunnel as preserved LNER A3 Pacific No.4472 Flying Scotsman *emerges into the Vale of Edale with a railtour to Sheffield and York on 29th September 1979.*
(Gavin Morrison)

The scenery of the Hope Valley line is apparent in this view taken just west of Edale on 3rd October 1959 with BR Class 2 2-6-0 No.78023 heading away from the station into the Vale of Edale with the 12.50pm Sheffield Midland—Chinley local service. In the background the hills rise to Broadlee Bank Tor and on up to Kinder Scout. (Michael Mensing)

A mixture of new and old on the 5.25pm Hope—Chinley local on Whit Sunday 17th May 1964. BR/Brush Type 2 (later Class 31) No.D5636 represents modern traction but the non-corridor compartment stock is very traditional. The location is approaching Chinley East Junction. (Michael Mensing)

Leaving Totley Tunnel, the second longest in Britain, BR Class 31 No.31 442 wheels MkII stock through Grindleford station with the 15.38 Sheffield—Liverpool on Sunday 15th May 1988, the last day of Class 31 working on these trains. (Gavin Morrison)

The south-to-east curve at Chinley was removed and then reinstated by BR in the early 1980s to enable limestone traffic from the Peak Forest line to run directly on to the Hope Valley line without a time-consuming reversal. Here Class 45 No.45 059 is bringing a train from Peak Forest across Chinley East Junction on 24th May 1984. (Gavin Morrison)

1980 saw the 150th anniversary of the historic Liverpool & Manchester Railway celebrated over three days in May by a cavalcade of locomotives at the site of the Rainhill Trials. The event saw a range of fascinating engine movements and this procession was recorded on the Chinley north curve on 29th May 1980. Two National Collection locomotives, MR 4-2-2 No.673 and LMS 4F 0-6-0 No.4027, with a steam crane and support vehicles, are returning via the Hope Valley to the Midland Railway Centre at Butterley; due to a fire risk during a lengthy period of hot and dry weather, they are being piloted by Class 25 diesel locomotive No.25 217. Note the newly-reinstated curve coming in to Chinley East Junction. (Gavin Morrison)

An uncharacteristically clean WD 2-8-0 No.90055 clanks through Edale station with a train of empty coal wagons from Gowhole on 3rd October 1959. (Michael Mensing)

LMS 4F 0-6-0 No.44134 toils westwards away from Hope station with a freight on 3rd October 1959. With the cab engulfed in steam, conditions look grim and it seems as if the crew is contending with a burst gauge glass. (Michael Mensing)

Just north west of Hope station are Earle's Sidings from where a short branch serves the Blue Circle Cement Works, one of many industrial sites grafted into the Peak District. BR Class 56 Co-Co No. 56 059 roars past the semaphore signals with an oil train on 27th March 1986.
(Gavin Morrison)

Winters can be harsh in the Peak District and blizzard conditions prevail at Hathersage station on 14th January 1987 as a two-car Class 101 diesel unit forming a Manchester—Sheffield service crunches gingerly along snow-covered rails. (Dr. L.A. Nixon)

A low winter sun highlights some vivid colours at Chinley North Junction in 1954 as LMS 'Jubilee' 4-6-0 No.45618 New Hebrides, its exhaust being whipped away by a stiff wind, heads a Hope Valley local from Manchester Central to Sheffield. The train has clear signals to take the left-hand divergence at the junction while a mineral train, with its locomotive blowing off, is held at the slow line signals. Cracken Edge dominates the skyline. (W. Oliver/Colour-Rail BRM1000)

LMS Fowler 2-6-4T No.42379 calls at Edale station on 22nd April 1961 during a fascinating tour organized jointly by the Stephenson and Manchester Locomotive Societies. Starting from Matlock, passengers went by bus to Cromford Wharf, there boarding wagons to ride the Cromford & High Peak line. Passenger stock was waiting at Friden and took the travellers to Hindlow and Old Harpur, then via Buxton and Peak Forest out to Edale. After reversal, the train terminated at Chinley. Those were the days! (Colour Rail)

High days at Wirksworth! On September 7th 1961 four preserved locomotives were taken up the branch from Derby Works to be filmed for the splendid TV series Railway Roundabout. *Featured here is Midland Railway 2-4-0 No.158A, built to the designs of Matthew Kirtley in 1866. All four locomotives survive to this day as part of the National Collection, the other three glamorous arrivals at Wirksworth being the Midland 4-2-2 No.118, the London, Tilbury & Southend 4-4-2T* Thundersley *and the Midland Compound No.1000 which was in steam and provided the motive power for the occasion.* (Colour Rail)

The proximity of the Wirksworth branch to Derby made it a most suitable line for the testing of diesel multiple units newly constructed at the Works there. In May 1959 an immaculate new unit, complete with 'cat's whiskers' and destined for service out of St. Pancras, has successfully completed the run from Derby and stands in the sun at Wirksworth. (Ray Oakley/Colour Rail DE2175)

THE CROMFORD & HIGH PEAK

Of all the Peak District's railway byways, none was weirder nor more wonderful than the Cromford & High Peak line. Who would build a railway over such mountainous terrain — and why? The answer to the latter was to connect the Cromford Canal with the Peak Forest Canal at Whaley Bridge in an area rich with limestone but with poor road communication for the transport of minerals or coal. The answer to the former was the engineer Josias Jessop who tackled the hills by building straight up them by means of nine rope-worked inclines. Its extemities at Cromford and Whaley Bridge were 227ft and 517ft above sea level respectively but between them the railway reached a summit at Ladmanlow of 1,266ft.

The High Peak Railway Act was passed on 2nd May 1825 and allowed the use of "any sufficient motive power". The line was opened from Cromford wharf to Hurdlow on 29th May 1830 and from Hurdlow to Whaley Bridge on 7th July 1831. Away from the inclines horses were employed and a journey from end to end took up to two days, goods only being carried. The first locomotive was obtained in 1833 and in 1853 a connection was made to the Midland at Cromford. In 1855 the railway obtained powers to carry passengers and to build a connection (opened in 1857) to the Stockport, Disley & Whaley Bridge Railway at the last-mentioned. A passenger service was provided using a brake vehicle with seats, though passengers were supposed to walk up and down the inclines; it was abandoned in 1877 after a fatality.

By 1857 the status of the Cromford & High Peak as a small independent company looked increasingly unrealistic in a growing national system and it wanted to seek powers to sell to the London & North Western, the Midland, the Stockport, Disley & Whaley Bridge or the Manchester, Sheffield & Lincolnshire "singly or together". In the end, as a result of negotiations the LNWR took a lease of the CHP on 25th March 1861 and later fully absorbed it in 1878. Thus it was that this 'up hill and down dale' oddity became part of the empire of the mighty 'Premier Line' whose principal route was the main line from London to Carlisle!

Horse traction had ended in 1871 apart from on the Whaley Bridge incline; a horse gin was used there until it closed in 1952 on account of a low bridge which precluded locomotive use. In 1869 the 1 in 16 Hurdlow incline was dispensed with when a deviation was opened with a modest maximum of just 1 in 41.

The LNWR's construction of a route from Buxton to join the North Staffordshire Railway at Ashbourne had considerable effect on the future of the Cromford & High Peak line. The stretch between Hindlow and Parsley Hay was reconstructed as part of the new line and from 25th June 1892 the CHP was abandoned between Ladmanlow and Shallcross as an easier route from Whaley Bridge now existed via Buxton. After the opening of the Buxton—Hindlow route, a new connection was provided from the latter to the remaining old section of the CHP at Harpur Hill on which quarries and limeworks were served; the Government also sited its Safety in Mines Research station at Old Harpur. The railway continued to Ladmanlow where a branch came in from Grin Low limestone quarries.

On the opening of the Buxton—Parsley Hay section a passenger coach was added to the rear of goods trains between Parsley Hay and Middleton Top, though passengers were again expected to alight and walk the inclines. This ended on completion of the Ashbourne line.

The course of the CHP in its desolate moorland setting almost defies description but it was dominated by its rope inclines which are listed below:

Incline	Length	Gradient
Cromford[1]	580yds	1 in 9
Sheep Pasture[1]	711yds	1 in 8
Middleton	708yds	1 in 8½
Hopton	457yds	1 in 14
Hurdlow[2]	850yds	1 in 16
Bunsall[3]	660yds	1 in 7½
Bunsall[3]	455yds	1 in 7
Shallcross[4]	817yds	1 in 10¼
Whaley Bridge[5]	180yds	1 in 13½

1. Combined 1857
2. Abandoned 1869
3. Combined 1857, abandoned 1892
4. Abandoned 1892
5. Abandoned 1952

The Hopton incline was the steepest adhesion-worked gradient in Britain, though it was originally operated by stationary engine and chain. At first it included 500 yards at 1 in 14 but the gradient was later eased by building up the approach embankment so that only 50-60yds at the top were at that, the rest being at a comparatively modest 1 in 60, 1 in 30 and 1 in 20. Another remarkable feature was Gotham curve which had a radius of just 55yds and because of which only four-wheeled wagons were allowed south of Friden.

Most traffic was local, though stone from the Hopton quarries went all over the country and there was a daily milk train between Buxton and Longcliffe. Some of the traffic was purely to provide the railway with its means of operating; for example, water was brought up from Cromford in tanks for the Sheep Pasture incline winding engine, while wood for the boilers on the Middleton incline was delivered daily from Derby Carriage & Wagon Works.

Traffic remained heavy into the 1950s. The Sheep Pasture incline winding engine was replaced by a new electric one in 1957, a sign of confidence as was the replacement of steam traction by a 204hp diesel shunter on the section between Sheep Pasture Top and Middleton Bottom in August 1966. On the upper section between Middleton and Friden a 350hp diesel was tried without success in 1966 and ex-War Department J94 0-6-0 saddle tanks (first introduced on the CHP in 1956) remained in charge.

However, as the railway entered the 1960s there came a decline in traffic as a result of quarry closures and growing road competition. With British Railways set upon modernization and the cutting out of uneconomic operations, the CHP's future was cast into doubt. The Middleton incline closed on 12th August 1963; the one engine allocated to the shed at Middleton was working a service on Mondays, Wednesdays and Fridays only, but there was increasingly little traffic. The end of the CHP was by then inevitable and the Middleton—Friden section closed on 30th April 1967 with farewell visits by a number of enthusiasts' groups; regular services had ceased the week before on 21st April. The Friden—Parsley Hay section closed in September that year, although it was not until six years later in September 1973 that the last piece of the CHP — from Hillhead Quarry to Harpur Hill and Hindlow Junction — was finally abandoned.

After closure Derbyshire County Council and the Peak District National Park purchased the trackbed between Cromford wharf and Hurdlow. Today the remarkable course of the CHP can be enjoyed by walkers on what is now the 'High Peak Trail' — but for many the winding of wagons up and down precipitous inclines or the hard-working tank engines charging gallantly at the steepest gradients on the railway system remain the abiding images of the most eccentric of the Peak District byways.

Some unlikely locomotives have found their way to the Cromford & High Peak line. During the late 1870s and 1880s LNWR 'Crewe Goods' 2-4-0s were used between Parsley Hay and the Middleton Incline and here is No.3083 at Hurdlow Top. The photograph was taken between 1887 when it was given this number and 1892 when it was withdrawn. Note the old tenders brought up daily to provide water for locomotives and local cottages. (NRM/LGRP 19909)

In 1876 the LNWR introduced a class of 50 2-4-0Ts for local passenger work. The first were withdrawn back in 1895 and most had gone by the turn of the century. Although eleven made it into LMS days, by 1936 the class had been reduced to one remarkable survior. Originally LNWR No.2278, it became LMS No.6428 (later 26428) and bravely soldiered on alone into the BR era when it acquired the number 58092, working on the Cromford & High Peak line between Sheep Pasture and Middleton Inclines from which it was finally withdrawn in 1952. No.6428 is pictured at Steeple Grange in September 1943. (Colour-Rail LM7)

The North London Railway, with its compact system operating suburban passenger trains and short-haul goods, was a wholly tank engine railway. For goods it relied on 0-6-0 tanks introduced by J.C. Park in 1879. Fifteen were taken over from the LMS by BR, the last holding out until 1960 a long way from home on the Cromford & High Peak line. In 1943 another exile based at Rowsley, LMS No.27527, contemplates a moorland setting at Middleton far from the chimney pots and docks of its home area. Built at Bow Works in 1900, it was withdrawn in 1957. (Colour-Rail LM8)

The first of the LMS Kitson-built oF 0-4-0STs No.47000 reposes outside the engine shed at Sheep Pasture in 1957. The little shed, with its almost ecclesiastical arched windows, is resplendent after a recent repaint — not so its occupant! (K. Cooper/Colour-Rail BRM1606)

North London 0-6-0T No.58860 (still with LMS lettering but with BR number) takes the spring air outside the corrugated iron engine shed at Middleton Top on 5th June 1950. All rainwater here was drained into a pit from which it ran into a reservoir; the winding engine then pumped it into a tank. This was necessary because all other water supplies had to be brought in converted tenders from Cromford. (T.J. Edgington)

Two water tenders prepare to ascend the Middleton Incline to provide supplies for the locomotive shed and winding engine at the top. (T.J. Edgington collection)

The Sheep Pasture Incline rose on a gradient of 1 in 9 increasing to 1 in 8 for a distance of 1,320 yards. Towards the bottom of the incline the tracks pass on either side of a catch pit for runaway wagons. This is the view from the A6 on 20th April 1947. (T.J. Edgington)

LNWR Webb-designed 2-4-0T No.58092 finished its long working life in 1952 on the Sheep Pasture—Middleton stretch of the line, yet this 'Chopper' tank (as they were known) had been built in 1877 for local passenger work! On 5th June 1950 it was photographed at Black Rocks, just west of Sheep Pasture Top. (T.J. Edgington)

NLR tank No.58860 rounds the sharp Minninglow curve with the 9.25am goods from Middleton Top to Friden on 5th June 1950. At this point the railway crossed the most impressive of a number of substantial limestone-faced embankments.
(T.J. Edgington)

The J94 0-6-0 saddle tanks first appeared on the Cromford & High Peak in 1956 and remained until the end. As its crew take a break in the autumn sunshine, No.68013 waits at Cromford Wharf in September 1963, its rusty bunker indicative of a hard life up in the Derbyshire hills. A fine LNWR signal looks down on the scene.
(D.J. Mitchell/Colour-Rail BRM1779)

The LNWR 'Chopper' tank was replaced by 0-4-0 saddle tank No.47000, one of five short wheelbase shunters purchased by the LMS in 1932 from Kitson & Co. It is seen at the bottom of the Middleton Incline in April 1953. (T.J. Edgington collection)

British Railways added to the LMS 0-4-0STs with another five of its own in 1953, all built at Horwich and with larger bunkers and smaller tanks. No.47006 of this version is at Sheep Pasture on 21st March 1964. Note the fireirons slung on the tank side and the attempt to impart a dash of style by painting the wheel rims. Cromford, Middleton and Sheep Pasture sheds were out-stations of Rowsley depot, but it 1964 that too lost its separate status and became a sub-shed of Derby. (Gavin Morrison)

OPPOSITE, TOP: *The eccentricity of the CHP line made it popular with railway enthusiasts, with special tours in open wagons and brake vans being organized. An excursion arranged by the publishers Ian Allan Ltd. on 25th September 1955 saw North London tanks Nos.58860 and 58850 charging up Hopton Incline with four wagonloads of passengers and two brake vans. The very last trains, on 30th April 1967, carried enthusiasts on farewell visits.*
(T.J. Edgington)

LOWER: *The last impressions of steam on the CHP are of the ex-War Department J94 0-6-0STs which first appeared in 1956. No.68006 is crossing the Minninglow embankment with a 'freight' from Middleton to Friden in April 1966. By this time traffic was at a very low ebb with a train running on some occasions, as here, just to collect the staff pay! Note the wooden doors fitted to the top of the cab to provide greater protection from the elements.*
(Dr. L.A. Nixon)

THIS PAGE, TOP: *Although the section between Ladmanlow and Burbage was abandoned in 1892, a visit on 15th May 1977 found the course easily traced on the approach to Burbage Tunnel.* (T.J. Edgington)

LOWER: *Exploration of the route of the CHP on 14th May 1977 found the remains of a wagon still residing in the catch pit on the Sheep Pasture Incline, a legacy of a runaway on 28th September 1965.* (T.J. Edgington)

Buxton is one of the highest towns in England, standing some 1,100ft above sea level in the Derbyshire moors. Originally a Roman settlement, it developed as a health resort on the strength of its spa waters and, notwithstanding its lofty situation and sometimes bleak climate, it established a fashionable reputation. It was clearly a destination railway companies would wish to reach.

There were various early schemes which never progressed beyond preliminary proposals; the Manchester & Birmingham Railway envisaged a line to Buxton and the grandly-titled Manchester, Buxton, Matlock and Midlands Junction Railway was formed in 1845. However, the origins of the present branch date from the Stockport, Disley & Whaley Bridge Railway which obtained powers in 1854 for a branch leaving the Manchester—Crewe line at Edgeley Junction in Stockport, despite objections from the Manchester, Sheffield & Lincolnshire Railway and the Midland Railway which both had ideas of reaching Buxton.

On 9th June 1857 the Stockport—Whaley Bridge line was opened and at the latter place gave connection with the Cromford & High Peak Railway which five years later was leased by the London & North Western. The next obvious development was to continue to Buxton and the SDWBR Extension Act was passed in July 1857, though it was two years before construction began. Passenger traffic on the Buxton Extension began on 15th June 1863. The powerful LNWR had been a supporter of the SDWB line and worked it from its opening, formally absorbing it on 16th November 1866.

The Midland Railway was also making its way to Buxton from a junction on its Derby—Manchester main line at Millers Dale. As the two Buxton stations were going to be adjacent to one another, the two owning companies agreed that they should be similar in design. However, agreement as to the nature of the design proved elusive and Sir Joseph Paxton, who was a Midland director and had designed the famous Crystal Palace for the Great Exhibition, was called in to advise on the final plans. The result was a pair of matching stone buildings, both having attractive semi-circular fan lights in the end walls around which were carved the names of the respective owning companies. After the formation of the LMSR at the 1923 grouping the two termini were regarded as one for administrative purposes with one station master and the platforms numbered consecutively — 1-3 in the LNWR building, 4-6 on the Midland side.

Once connected to the railway network, Buxton's population grew steadily and doubled during the twentieth century as the town both flourished as an inland resort and became a popular residence for Manchester businessmen. The LNWR route provided a slightly quicker service than was possible via the Midland.

On 26th May 1885 a curve at Middlewood from the North Staffordshire Railway's Marple—Macclesfield route to the Buxton line was opened jointly by the LNWR and NSR. Whilst its main advantage lay in providing the facility to work freights between the two lines, it also enabled the LNWR to run through coaches from London Euston to Buxton via Macclesfield during the summer season. The NSR also offered a seasonal Macclesfield—Buxton service.

However, the severe gradients caused operating difficulties for freight traffic and it was on a freight train that the Buxton's line's most notorious incident took place. On 9th February 1957 LMS 8F 2-8-0 No.48188 was working an unfitted freight from Buxton when the steam brake pipe in the cab fractured. The cab was engulfed in scalding steam and the crew had to retreat to the steps outside the cab. The train was soon running away out of control on the 1 in 58/1 in 60 gradient from Dove Holes towards Whaley Bridge in spite of the crew's valiant efforts to stop or at least slow it by attempting to shut the regulator using fireirons. Fireman Ron Scanlon was instructed by the driver, John Axon, to jump from the engine and try to drop the brake handles on the wagons as they passed him, but the train was going too fast for him to have much success. Driver Axon bravely remained on the locomotive clinging to the cab from the outside while striving to close the regulator which was still open from the climb out of Buxton. At Chapel-en-le-Frith South station the train crashed into the back of another freight, killing its guard. Driver Axon also lost his life and for his gallantry was posthumously awarded the George Cross, while Fireman Scanlon was awarded £50 for his efforts. The events were subsequently commemorated in one of the acclaimed BBC 'radio ballads', *The Ballad of John Axon*. The difficulty of working freight on the line saw it diverted to the Midland route in 1963.

The *Reshaping of British Railways* report in 1963 envisaged closure of both the Buxton lines but a vigorous campaign by users of the LNWR route was effective in persuading the Minister of Transport that the volume of commuter traffic could not be accommodated on the roads. A reprieve for the Stockport to Buxton line was granted in June 1964 and today modern 'Sprinter' diesel trains provide a frequent service to and from Manchester Piccadilly, covering the journey in around 55 minutes.

The Midland's main line over the Peak required a lengthy tunnel at Dove Holes but the LNWR, climbing steadily in the Buxton direction at 1 in 60 towards the summit beyond Dove Holes station, passes through the modest 431 yards of Eaves Tunnel. Emerging into Barmoor Clough is LMS 2-6-4T No.42599 with the 10.20am from Manchester on 22nd April 1951. (E.R. Morten)

Near Chapel-en-le-Frith the LNWR Buxton line crossed the Midland main line to Derby which burrowed through the embankment by way of Chapel LNW Tunnel. An 8F 2-8-0 is heading a freight from Buxton on 10th February 1962. (Alan Tyson collection)

South of Dove Holes, some 1,100ft above sea level, is Bibbington's Sidings, site of a lime works established there when the railway opened. An 8F 2-8-0, shrouded in steam, grinds towards the summit on the climb (mostly at 1 in 66) from Buxton with a train of ICI hoppers diverted from the MR route on Sunday 23rd January 1955. A banking engine is pushing at the rear. "It's a seven-mile drop from Bibbington top" according to the line in The Ballad of John Axon and it was here, just over three years later, that the drama of the runaway train began which culminated in the death of Driver Axon. (E.R. Morten)

The damaged front end of 8F No.48188 at Chapel-en-le-Frith South presents a sorry sight after being removed from the wreckage of the accident on 9th February 1957. After running away out of control with a freight from Buxton due to the fracture of the steam brake pipe, it had crashed into the rear of another goods train in Chapel station. (Colour-Rail)

A pair of three-car Birmingham Railway Carriage & Wagon Co. diesel multiple units forms the 4.25pm Buxton—Manchester Piccadilly near Lyme Park, Disley, on Sunday 5th April 1964. Lyme Park, with its Elizabethan house, grounds and deer park, was served by Disley station and has long been a popular day-out destination from the Manchester area. (Michael Mensing)

LNWR 'Prince of Wales' 4-6-2T No. 6963, resplendent in LMS crimson lake livery, stands at a snowy Buxton station c1924. LNWR livery still prevails on the leading brake vehicle of its Manchester train. (E.R. Morten)

LMS Fowler 2-6-4T No.42366 stands in the LNWR station at Buxton waiting to depart with the 4.29pm to Manchester London Road on 18th July 1955. (T.J. Edgington)

The end screen of the LNWR building photographed on 30th August 1986, with the company name in the stonework around the fanlight. (T.J. Edgington)

The LNWR opened a new six-road engine shed at Buxton in 1892 and it must have been one of the most exposed on the system. After the closure of the small Midland shed in 1935, locomotives of that company's origin began to be based at the North Western depot, witness Johnson 0-4-4T No.58083 on 6th July 1956, fitted with push-pull apparatus for working the Buxton—Millers Dale service. (Gavin Morrison)

BUXTON TO ASHBOURNE

The last of the railways to be built in the Peak District came very late in the nineteenth century as a result of the LNWR's desire to gain access to the still-growing spa town of Buxton from the south.

Its origins, though, lie with another railway company, the North Staffordshire Railway, which in 1852 had opened a branch from Rocester, on its Churnet Valley line, to Ashbourne. The LNWR had running powers over the NSR and also over the Midland Railway's line from Burton-on-Trent to Nuneaton, so a link from Ashbourne to Buxton would give it a route all the way from Euston.

In 1887 the LNWR obtained powers for the Buxton & High Peak Junction Railway, a five-mile route which left Buxton curving away to the south to join the Cromford & High Peak (of which the LNWR was the lessee) near Hindlow. This was opened in 1892 but two years before, the LNWR had obtained powers for the Buxton & Ashbourne Railway to run from Parsley Hay to meet the NSR at Ashbourne.

The Buxton—Parsley Hay section, which involved upgrading and re-aligning part of the Cromford & High Peak route, was opened to passengers on 1st June 1894 but construction beyond the latter place did not begin until 1896; perhaps the LNWR had lost some of its enthusiasm for the engineering work involved in building a line which offered little prospect of much local trade. There were limestone quarries, though, and the LNWR pressed ahead over the next three years until the branch was at last opened on 4th June 1899.

The Buxton—Ashbourne line passed through a remote landscape of Peak District moorland and a good deal of civil engineering was needed to achieve it. The route began at Buxton with a fifteen-arch viaduct, then another over Duke's Drive of thirteen arches. On the realignment of the former CHP section between Hindlow and Parsley Hay a 514yds tunnel was driven at Hindlow, there were numerous limestone cuttings, a seven-arch viaduct over the Bradbourne Brook and a 378yds tunnel on the approach to Ashbourne.

Double track was provided between Buxton and Parsley Hay, with intermediate stations at Higher Buxton, Hindlow and Hurdlow. Beyond Parsley Hay the line was single track to Ashbourne, with stations and passing loops at Hartington, Alsop-en-le-Dale, Tissington and Thorpe Cloud. During construction, however, allowance had been optimistically made for the track to be doubled in the future if the need arose — it never did.

The opening of the branch from Ashbourne provided the LNWR with a more direct route from London Euston to Buxton and through services could be run routed from Nuneaton via Ashby and Burton-on-Trent by virtue of its running powers over the NSR and MR and joint ownership with the Midland of the Ashby & Nuneaton Joint Railway. This routing superseded the previous use of the Middlewood curve to approach Buxton from the north via Disley. The LNWR offered a first class tourist return fare of £2 3s 4d [£2.17] and a journey time of 4hr 24min, but the Great War put an end to these operations.

Despite the above, the Buxton—Ashbourne line never rose above branch line status as far as passenger traffic was concerned, hardly surprising given the sparsely-populated terrain it traversed. Even by 1950s standards it was held to be uneconomic and passenger services between Buxton and Uttoxeter were withdrawn from 1st November 1954.

Occasional excursions — and even emergency passenger trains during severe winter snow — lingered on until 1963. Limestone traffic was plentiful for some years but the line was declared closed between Ashbourne and Hartington on 7th October 1963. Hartington remained served by quarry traffic and by water tenders delivered to supply the railway houses but the line from there to Parsley Hay was closed on 2nd October 1967. The route beyond Parsley Hay hung on with the remaining part of the Cromford & High Peak line. Complete closure between Parsley Hay and Hindlow came on 21st November 1967, but the limestone quarries just south of Hindlow still keep the stretch of line from there to Buxton in use.

Those with stout footwear and a modest amount of energy can still enjoy the course of the line from Parsley Hay to Ashbourne — between 1968 and 1972 it was turned into the 'Tissington Trail' footpath!

Ashbourne station was jointly owned by the London & North Western and the North Staffordshire Railways. This pre-grouping view is from the south, looking towards Buxton. (T.J. Edgington collection)

Tissington station on 7th August 1953. Excursions for ramblers and for the famous well-dressing ceremony continued to use the station until May 1963. (H.C. Casserley)

A Railway Correspondence & Travel Society special from Sheffield on 27th June 1964 saw LNER B1 4-6-0 No.61360 running between Buxton and Parsley Hay, where passengers transferred to open wagons to travel on the Cromford & High Peak line. The train has just left Hindlow Tunnel on a section of the old CHP route reconstructed by the London & North Western Railway. The bleak moorland is typical of the sparsely-populated terrain through which the Ashbourne line passed. Note the sign instructing "Goods trains to stop and pin down brakes" on the falling gradient. (Gavin Morrison)

Between Ashbourne and Parsley Hay the line was single track with passing loops at all stations except Thorpe Cloud. Alsop-en-le-Dale enjoys a busy moment on 5th May 1962 as a pair of LNWR 0-8-0s Nos.49439 and 49281 meets in the station loop. No.49439, on the left heading south, has a tender cab, a facility which engine crews might appreciate in winter weather. (Alan Tyson collection)

Although the Ashbourne—Buxton line had lost its passenger service in 1954, Parsley Hay's wooden station was still intact on 5th May 1962 when LNWR G2 0-8-0 No.49439 was shunting the 9.00am Buxton to Uttoxeter goods. Note the shunting pole propped against the signal box and the signalman's motor cycle and sidecar on the platform. (Alan Tyson collection)

LNWR G2 0-8-0 No.49406 trudges up the climb out of Buxton with a goods for Uttoxeter on 23rd September 1961. In the windswept moorland field two sturdy cows watch its passing; the third, doubtless having seen it before, ignores it. (Michael Mensing)

There is no sign of life in this windswept landscape apart from English Electric Class 37s Nos.37 680 and 37 684 double-heading a train of limestone up the 1 in 60 gradient approaching Hindlow along the last remaining stretch of the Ashbourne line on 15th February 1989.
(Dr. L.A. Nixon)

Near Hindlow the wilderness impression is rudely shattered by the industrial sites at Briggs Sidings serving Hindlow Buxton Lime Industries and Dowlow Redland quarry. English Electric Class 40 No.40 192 prepares to depart for Buxton on 5th January 1984, passing an abandoned signal gantry. (Dr. L.A. Nixon)

THE PEAK FOREST TRAMWAY

The Peak Forest Tramway was a great survivor. It was opened in 1799 and worked, largely unchanged, until 1926. By that time it was owned by the London & North Eastern Railway and the Peak Forest's horse-drawn wagons must have contrasted starkly with the parent company's *Flying Scotsman*-hauled expresses! In 1846 the Peak Forest Canal and Tramway had both passed into the ownership of the Sheffield, Ashton-under-Lyne & Manchester Railway, soon to be a constituent of the Manchester, Sheffield & Lincolnshire and later the ambitious Great Central.

The Peak Forest Tramway was a classic example of the railway in its formative years. It was horse-powered, its principal traffic was limestone from the Derbyshire quarries (although it did bring in coal and general goods) and it served the Peak Forest Canal through the canal basin at Bugsworth, a village now generally referred to as Buxworth.

Benjamin Outram, a native Derbyshireman and one of the principal pioneers of the horse-drawn railway, built the Tramway. No mean canal engineer also, Outram was responsible for the longest canal tunnel on Britain's waterways, at Standedge on the Huddersfield Canal, and he was responsible for two other similar tramways in Derbyshire, at Little Eaton and Ticknall.

Outram surveyed the course of the tramway from the canal basin at Buxworth through Chapel-en-le-Frith to Dove Holes where branches served the various quarries. The line climbed about 600ft in seven miles, included a short tunnel at Stoddart and a 500yd-long inclined plane at Chapel-en-le-Frith. A second plane linked the original Outram line to quarries at Loads Knowl, near Dove Holes.

The Tramway was laid to a gauge of 4ft 2½in — seemingly the Outram 'standard' gauge. 'L'-shaped cast iron plate rails, 3ft in length, were used, seated on stone blocks. Where the line crossed a public road 'U'-section rail was used. In the 1860s the Manchester, Sheffield & Lincolnshire, by then owners of the Tramway, saw fit to renew the track with steel rails from its Gorton Works — but to the original design, of course! Such was the traffic on the Tramway in its early years that, with the exception of Stoddart Tunnel, the single line had been doubled by 1803.

The Tramway's original rolling stock was very basic, wooden wagons with iron body fittings and iron tyres. As traffic grew, wagons with iron bodies and wheels came into use, the wheels being of plain profile to be compatible with the track plates. The Tramway boasted three stables, at Dove Holes, Chapel-en-le-Frith and Buxworth, for its motive power. Horses worked in teams of five or two. Five horses hauled empties or loaded coal trains up the Tramway while a two-horse team sufficed for lighter loads such as wagons of corn. Each team was in charge of a waggoner assisted by a 'nipper', the latter a boy in his early teens. These two worthies took charge of the horses pulling wagons up the line and attempted to brake loaded stone trains descending under the impulse of gravity. Each wagon brake was two hooks joined by three links of chain; the waggoner fastened one hook to the wagon body and to slow the wagon the other hook was inserted between the spokes of the wheel — broken wheels, let alone broken limbs, must have been commonplace! By 1903 the Great Central Railway was paying waggoners 25 shillings (£1 25p) per week to undertake this risky occupation. Nippers received just 15 shillings (75p)

The inclined plane at Chapel-en-le-Frith was 'self-acting', that is to say that the loaded wagons descending the plane hauled the empties to the top. Hemp ropes and chains were used in the early days but finally a continuous wire rope provided an unbreakable solution.

The Peak Forest Tramway grew old gracefully. Steam power and the internal combustion engine took away its traffic and by 1926 the Tramway — unchanged in principle from its first day of operation — stood out of use.

One of its wagons is preserved in the National Railway Museum at York, a fitting reminder of how canals and railways combined to forge the Industrial Revolution.

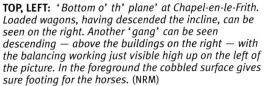

TOP, LEFT: *'Bottom o' th' plane' at Chapel-en-le-Frith. Loaded wagons, having descended the incline, can be seen on the right. Another 'gang' can be seen descending — above the buildings on the right — with the balancing working just visible high up on the left of the picture. In the foreground the cobbled surface gives sure footing for the horses.* (NRM)

TOP, RIGHT: *The canal basin at Buxworth, referred to in its heyday as 'Bugholes'. To the right of the warehouse stand wagons loaded with limestone and at the left of the picture is a curious frame and wheel structure. This was used to raise the tramway wagons so that their hinged end-doors opened and the limestone tipped into canal barges waiting below. In the early twentieth century Mr. Isaac Worth of Buxworth was employed as the operator of this splendid tipper.* (NRM)

LOWER, RIGHT: *Peak Forest Tramway wagon No.174 is now preserved at the National Railway Museum in York. Dating from 1797, it is the oldest vehicle in the National Collection. No.174 has had a long museum career and is seen here in the original York Railway Museum in 1927 — note the brake hooks hanging from the wagon side to the nearest wheel and the rudimentary plateway pointwork in the foreground.* (NRM)

PEAK DISTRICT NARROW GAUGE

The Peak District fostered two narrow gauge lines but they were as different as chalk and cheese. The Leek & Manifold Valley Light Railway came into the south west of the area. Constructed to the highest standards, it was a small piece of the Indian sub-continent transported to Staffordshire. In the north east, and in stark contrast, was the Ashover Light Railway, a transport arm of the Clay Cross Company. Built on the cheap with surplus equipment from the military railways of the Western Front, this line had a working life of less than 25 years.

The Leek & Manifold Valley Light Railway served the Staffordshire portion of the Peak. From its interchange with the standard gauge North Staffordshire Railway branch at Waterhouses the 2ft 6in gauge line traversed eight and a quarter miles of the remote Manifold Valley, serving hamlets and beauty spots such as Sparrowlee, Thor's Cave and Ecton before terminating at Hulme End — very much a rural retreat! There were rumours of an extension Buxton-wards but these came to nought.

The line was splendidly equipped, its engineer, E.R. Calthrop, saw to that. A passionate believer in the values of less-than-standard gauge railways, Calthrop had made a considerable success of the Barsi Light Railway in India, so it was hardly surprising that the lessons learnt there should be applied to the Leek & Manifold.

The total motive power of the line was two decidedly 'Indian-looking' 2-6-4 tanks. Named *E.R.Calthrop* and *J.B.Earle*, these were supplied by Kitson's of Leeds. Four saloon carriages, originally arrayed in a delightful primrose livery, provided the passenger accommodation and of the railway's eight goods wagons, five were transporters for the conveyance of standard gauge wagons up the narrow gauge. Where interchange traffic with the standard gauge was expected, the stations were provided with short spurs of track to accommodate the larger wagons — but overbridges had to be built to standard gauge size, thereby removing a narrow gauge advantage.

The line opened on 27th June 1904 and was operated from the start by the North Staffordshire Railway. After the initial excitement had died down, the L&M settled into a pattern of passenger service which saw it through its life. Two trains each way each day generally sufficed throughout the winter but this rose to three in summertime with extras at Bank Holidays and Wakes Weeks when the populace of the Potteries flocked into the great outdoors. At such times the goods wagons, fitted with seats and benches, formed adequate but inelegant passenger vehicles!

It had been hoped that a redevelopment of the lead and copper deposits at Ecton would provide a staple mineral traffic. This was not to be but in the early 1920s the opening of a creamery at Ecton demanded a daily service and the transporter wagons were able to prove their worth.

Although a splendid engineering achievement — the original 35lb per yard rails lasted the railway's lifetime — the Leek & Manifold was never a very sound financial proposition. From 1923 the line came under the control of the London, Midland & Scottish Railway and the bucolic ramblings of a minor narrow gauge line fitted uncomfortably with the hard-headed business strategies of Euston Square. By the early 1930s the developing motor bus services in the Staffordshire Peak served the villages much better than the L&M could ever hope to; after all, the buses went through the villages, which were on the valley sides and surrounding hill tops. The trains took a railway's traditional course — along the valley bottom with a brisk stroll up to one's final destination. The loss of the line's staple traffic with the closure of the Ecton creamery in 1932 proved the last straw and the Leek & Manifold closed completely on 10th March 1934. One of the transporter wagons found its way over to the Ashover Light Railway and *J.B. Earle* lingered for three years at Crewe Works before being cut up, while *E.R. Calthrop* was put briefly back into steam to assist with the removal of the track which was completed by October 1937. This locomotive was then cut up and the LMS turned the trackbed over to the Staffordshire County Council for use as a footpath, a function which it fulfils to this day.

The rural delights of the Leek & Manifold with J.B. Earle *and brake composite coach in the original primrose livery at Redhurst crossing. A platform for milk churns was added here in 1907 and a passenger halt opened in 1915 – the only instance of a new station being added on the L&M after its opening.* (NRM/LPC/LMV1)

Hulme End, the northern terminus of the Leek & Manifold, and even in the days of the LMS train crews had time to pose for photographs on the narrow gauge! It was originally envisaged that Hulme End would be the halfway point on the line as it extended north towards Buxton. The buildings to the right of the photograph are the engine and carriage sheds, located at the logical but never-to-be-realised mid-point of the line.
(T.J. Edgington collection)

E.R. Calthrop on shed at Hulme End in June 1924. A narrow gauge masterpiece, the locomotive is complete with large headlamp and rerailing jacks by the smokebox. Livery is the 1919 North Staffordshire Railway 'madder lake' – a sort of rusty red? – with a single cream line. (T.J. Edgington collection)

A standard gauge van on a transporter wagon towers over J.B.Earle at Hulme End in 1933. In the background another standard gauge wagon can be seen standing on one of the stubs of full-size track provided at stations on the L&M. The transporter wagons were supplied to the railway by the Cravens Railway Carriage & Wagon Company at an eventual price of £315 each.
(NRM/J.F. Bruton collection 19)

All ready for the trippers! At Waterhouses in 1933 two of the L&M's open wagons are pressed into service as the most rudimentary of coaches. These wagons were built by the Leeds Forge Company and were really intended to carry milk churns.
(T.J. Edgington collection)

The Ashover Light Railway had a short life but an interesting pedigree. The Clay Cross Company, founded by George Stephenson, promoted the line to exploit the mineral wealth of the Overton estate which it had purchased in 1918 and which lay near the village of Ashover. The engineer for the project was none other than Colonel H.F. Stephens, the doyen of light railway projects in the years following the Great War. The line, seven and a quarter miles long and built to the military gauge of 60cm or one foot eleven and five-eighths inches, described a leisurely 'S' linking the quarries of Ashover Butts and Fallgate with the Clay Cross Works in the industrial North East Derbyshire town.

The railway opened on 6th April 1925. By this time six Baldwin-built ex-War Department 4-6-0Ts were available for traffic. Their angular trans-Atlantic lines and increasingly erratic performance were offset by homely names: *Hummy*, *Guy*, *Joan*, *Peggy* and *Bridget*. These were the children of the chairman of the Clay Cross Company, General Thomas Jackson, and although there was supposed to have been a *Georgie* this name was never used and *Guy* was carried successively by Baldwins Nos.2 and 6. Passengers were carried in four Gloucester Railway Carriage & Wagon Works vehicles; in 1926 these were supplemented by a further eight coaches from the 'Neverstop Railway' of the previous year's Empire Exhibition at Wembley. Mineral traffic was catered for by 40 ex-WD wagons.

At first the prospects seemed bright, mineral traffic was robust and over 5,000 passengers were carried in the first week of operation. A service of eight daily return trips was expanded at weekends and holiday times as trippers used the little line to escape from coalfield Derbyshire to the sylvan delights of Ashover and the Amber Valley. Although the quarries were the real business objectives of the railway, the 'Where the Rainbow Ends' refreshment rooms at Ashover Butts proved a big draw, certainly to the likes of the author's mother on the annual Sunday School treat!

Alas it was all an illusion; the coal strike of 1926 plus the increasing competition from local buses — one driven by the author's uncle — soon ate into the passenger traffic. Winter services ceased in 1934 and all timetabled services were suspended in 1936. A few specials ran during the war years and the last trip over the whole line was a Birmingham Locomotive Club special in August 1947, four wagons hauled by *Joan*.

Mineral traffic continued in declining quantities over the ageing — and ailing — track. The steam locomotives were cannibalized in order that at least one or two should be serviceable and diesel traction appeared, including a home-made example from the Clay Cross Works.

With the fulfilment of the last mineral contract in March 1950, the line closed. A brief 25-year span brought an era to a close; given survival for another ten years, what might the wonders of preservation have wrought?

Pride in our train! Driver, fireman, guard and a couple of the passengers pose for a photograph at Ashover. Hummy, in plain black livery, was named for Henry Humphrey Jackson, the second son of the company chairman; the carriages are half the original Gloucester Railway Carriage & Wagon Company order, a mere £817 the pair, delivered at Clay Cross.
(T.J. Edgington collection)

The industrial origins of the Ashover Light Railway are evident as Joan stands at the Clay Cross end of the line September 1930. The full name of the terminus was Clay Cross and Egstow and the small timber station sat almost directly above the northern end of the LMS Clay Cross Tunnel, the coal seams found in which gave rise to the Clay Cross Company in George Stephenson's day.
(T.J. Edgington collection)

Ashover Butts station in March 1948. Stone trains still run from the Butts Quarry, quarter of a mile over the cameraman's shoulder but the Butts chapel overlooks a melancholy scene. The 'Where the Rainbow ends' café was just up the bank off the left of the picture and in 1925 a return from Clay Cross to the country terminus would have cost 10d.
(T.J. Edgington collection)

Ashover Butts a few months earlier in August 1947 with enthusiasts from Birmingham and Manchester enjoying a last run over the line. The locomotive Joan is much decayed from her earliest days on the railway when she sported a livery of crimson lake lined out in black and yellow. (T.J. Edgington)

Joan takes water at Fallgate with the 'last special' on 24th August 1947 – a nice example of Ashover 'make do and mend'. The whole excursion seems to have cost a grand total of £9; the organisers were told "don't hurry … try and be back by teatime" and rumours persist that, on a hot day, the Miner's Arms at Milltown was drunk dry! (T.J. Edgington)